CountryLiving

Mini Makeovers

CountryLiving

Mini Makeovers

EASY WAYS TO TRANSFORM EVERY ROOM

HEARST
books

HEARST BOOKS

An Imprint of Sterling Publishing Co., Inc.
1166 Avenue of the Americas
New York, NY 10036

ISBN 978-1-61837-250-5

Distributed in Canada by Sterling Publishing
c/o Canadian Manda Group, 664 Annette Street
Toronto, Ontario, M6S 2C8, Canada
Distributed in Australia by NewSouth Books
45 Beach Street, Coogee, NSW 2034, Australia

For information about custom editions, special sales, and premium and corporate
purchases, please contact Sterling Special Sales at 800-805-5489
or specialsales@sterlingpublishing.com.

Manufactured in China

2 4 6 8 10 9 7 5 3 1

sterlingpublishing.com
countryliving.com

Cover design by Chris Thompson
Interior design by Sharon Jacobs
Photography credits on page 222

Contents

Every so often, it's time for a change—little updates that refresh a room, yet make a big impact. These micro-decorating moves can be simple, like buying new throw pillows for a couch, or rearranging a collection to provide visual impact in a room, or a weekend project, like a fresh coat of paint for your walls or kitchen cabinets. But that's as far as the heavy lifting goes—which isn't so very far in terms of the time or energy required. After all, these are mini makeovers—no major remodeling or time commitment necessary.

At *Country Living*, we're all about the idea that decorating should be fun and easy, it doesn't have to cost much, and great old things can and should be put to wonderful new uses (hello, flea-market finds!). And we're not going to lie—we enjoy spending a couple of hours on an uncomplicated craft. That's why, throughout this book, you'll find callouts for things you can create ("Make it!"), things you can upcycle ("Reuse it!") and things you can snap up for a song ("Bargain!"). And you'll find ideas for every room in the house, from the entryway to the mudroom. (If you don't have a mudroom find out how to fake one on page 212.) *Get ready to be inspired to make over your home, one easy idea at a time.*

Rachel Barrett

RACHEL HARDAGE BARRETT
EDITOR IN CHIEF
Country Living

UMPQUA

ECONOMY MARKET
GEO. KOHLHAGEN

Make it!

Signage from a great-grandfather's butcher shop and gold-leaf frame that contains photo booth pictures the family takes every year at the country fair make this hearth uniquely personal.

CHAPTER 1

Living Rooms

M of us focus our best decorating efforts on the living room. After all, it's the space visitors are likeliest to see. And who doesn't want their home to make a great first impression? But even the most carefully designed room eventually needs a little lift—rugs and furniture wear, styles change, and sometimes, you just want to switch things up. The good news is change is easy! Slipcovers can restore worn upholstery for a fraction of the cost of new furniture. Throw pillows in trendy colors or patterns can update instantly. Artwork can be rearranged, and suddenly you'll see it—and your living room—in a different light. Or go big! Swap your wall color for something completely different—say, an unexpected charcoal hue. Cover your plain white ceiling paint with an airy pale-blue shade. The possibilities are endless, and you have to do only a little to get a lot of satisfaction.

Buy it!

A mix of patterned pillows adds visual interest to this sunny, inviting room.

Pretty Pillows

Make it!

Feminine floral prints give neutral furniture a fresh-from-the-garden makeover. You can make a 16 × 16-inch throw pillow with only a yard of fabric!

Ever wondered why your beautiful new couch looks so naked right after it's delivered and installed in your living room? You've discovered firsthand the magic of throw pillows.

Small and seemingly insignificant, these delightful bits of puff can transform a bland room, making it welcoming, pulled together, on trend, and comfortable in one fell swoop. And you don't have to spend a lot. Off-price retail stores like HomeGoods® and T.J. Maxx® are great resources, as are websites like Etsy®. For a high-end look without a high price, search out vendors who make pillows using leftover pieces of to-the-trade fabrics or antique rugs. Don't be afraid to mix patterns (though sticking to just a couple of color families works best). Florals and stripes are classic country choices, and solid colors can make a bold statement. Choosing neutral-colored furniture gives you the most options—you can punch up the room with patterns and bright hues, or stick with beiges (like the grain-sack pillows on page 11) to create a serene vibe. Throws pick up where pillows leave off, adding coziness and—depending on what you choose—color, pattern, and texture.

Buy it! The pillows in this understated living room enhance the room's ambience and take it one step further. They share the nubby texture of the French postal sack framed above the couch and pick up the striped pattern of the armchair, while introducing one of the few pops of color.

Buy it! A resolutely practical brown sofa provides the perfect backdrop for an assortment of bright pillows. Paired with the equally striking artwork above the couch, they bring big personality to an otherwise humdrum room.

Fabric Magic

New upholstery, slipcovers, or curtains can change a room in an instant, in all kinds of ways. Re-covering a group of chairs in the same fabric can make them appear to be a matching set (even if they're not), giving a room some polish. The fabric you choose depends on both the space and the mood you want to create. Bold, large-scale prints would feel loud in a white living room like the one on page 16, but a subtle pattern, such as a thin brown pinstripe, is just right. The hearty denim-blue upholstery on the chairs on this page couldn't be more in sync with the refined, time-worn vibe of the vintage rug and weathered side and coffee tables. To evoke a farmhouse feeling, head straight for buffalo checks and flowered chintz, classic patterns that telegraph down-home tradition. Fabric with vertical stripes can make a bold statement when it's used in curtains. To give the ceiling a visual lift, mount rods above the window frames.

Do it!

These four chairs are upholstered in the same fabric (with contrasting cushion seats), but they're not a set. Look closely: Two are 1940s American chairs, and two are French Art Deco.

Do it!

Baby-blue buffalo-check fabric covers on the seat pillows of a vintage cane-back sofa take it down a notch from formal to friendly. Pretty blue-and-white pillows are comfortable and welcoming.

Do it!

Understated brown stripes on the slipcovers of a club chair set are the perfect match for a light, airy space.

Bargain! The upholstery on this fancy 9-foot-long French sofa? Durable, affordable painter's drop cloths! The neutral color helps it blend in rather than overpower the small living room. Plus, the hardy fabric will hold up to the wear and tear of everyday living.

Know Your

STRIPES

TICKING
This tightly woven cotton or linen was first used on mattresses.

GRAIN SACK
A distinctive stripe helped farmers identify their sacks easily.

PINSTRIPE
This narrow stripe is often used in men's suiting.

Buy it!

Curtains with vertical green stripes break up the horizontal lines created by the room's pine-board paneling, add a feeling of height, and are a stunning addition to the room. The linear theme is carried out by the bold rug, the sofa pillows, and a green chair with a wide white stripe made by applying fabric paint right down the middle.

Unexpected Accents

Choosing the right basic pieces for your living room is important, but after that, it's time to search out objects with a surprise factor. Whether they're vintage curiosities, repurposed industrial pieces, or timeworn favorites that have taken a new twist, these are the items that give a room *your* personality. Online secondhand stores, flea markets, even your own attic or garage—they're all happy hunting grounds.

Bargain!

This galvanized cart lived its first life in a restaurant kitchen. The homeowner snapped it up for just $100, and now it has pride of place in the living room, where it displays a collection of precious odds and ends.

The homeowner's childhood piano was updated with chalk paint, which gives it a thick finish with a matte look. Tempted to try? Here's encouragement: It requires virtually zero sanding or priming.

Grab a Seat

Simple slipcovers can give living room chairs a boost, but you don't have to stop there. Re-cover the seat pillows in a contrasting fabric, or tuck in a fluffy flokati sheepskin for extra comfort and warmth. If you're short on seating when company comes, pick up a pouf or two. When your guests leave, tuck them out of the way, or use them as everyday accents. The grain-sack pouf on page 23 is a project anyone can tackle.

Do it!

Creamy flokati throws add softness to the seats of slip-covered armchairs and bring texture to the room.

Make it!

Need extra seating? You can create this handsome upholstered pouf in a flash!

Pouf

1. Starting with 3½ yards of grain-sack fabric, cut out nine 8½ × 26-inch rectangles, centering the stripes on each rectangle.

2. Sew the pieces right sides together along the long edges, creating a large rectangle. Fold the rectangle in half, right sides together, and then sew the remaining long edges together to create a tube. Turn the tube right side out. Fold a pleat 2 inches from the left-hand corner of each panel; tack down the pleat with a stitch. Repeat on other end of the panel.

3. Cut two circles of fabric 16 inches in diameter for the top and bottom of the pouf. Fold a ½-inch hem around the end of each circle. Using a running stitch, hand-sew one circle to one end of the tube, 1½ inches from the edge of the tube. Repeat with the second circle on the other end, leaving a small opening in the bottom for stuffing.

4. Stuff with beanbag filler, and hand-stitch the opening closed.

Coffee Tables

Swap out a run-of-the-mill coffee table for something one of a kind, and you'll immediately make your living room a most interesting place to be. Look for pieces that started out in life as something else—doors, windows, wagon wheels, chicken crates, cable spools, baskets. If you're up for a project, you can easily replace the glass in a conventional rectangular glass-topped metal coffee table (thrift stores are full of them) with slats of repurposed wood for an industrial-meets-country look.

Reuse it!

Casters turn an old pigeon basket into a woven conversation piece. Another simple accent that will update a room? Add a lemon tree, like the one beside the sofa!

Reuse it! An old storm door with eight beautifully weathered windowpanes serves as the top of this unusual coffee table.

Arranging a Coffee Table

~IN FOUR SIMPLE STEPS~

1 START WITH A PRETTY TRAY.

A piece that mimics the shape of your table helps organize items neatly and acts as a pretty layering element. Next, anchor the opposite corner with an oversize book to balance the tray. Illustrated books invite laid-back perusing.

2 ZERO IN ON THE REMAINING CORNERS.

Envision your table in quadrants, and aim for rough symmetry along the diagonals. Here, a stack of smaller books faces off with lidded boxes that corral necessary odds and ends: remotes, matches, cards, and more.

3 JUST ADD PERSONALITY.

Set out things that will spark curiosity and conversation, like a collection of glass bottles. Plus, you can top stacks with an interesting object, and then a large book or a pile of magazines becomes a pedestal.

4 FINISH WITH ORGANIC DETAILS.

Plants or flowers, such as the orchid placed off-center here, give life to any surface—literally! Don't overdo it; a coffee table should have plenty of space for cups of coffee!

Little Wonders

I f your living room is petite, regular-size furniture may be too intrusive. Creative solutions—such as a narrow bench pressed into service as a coffee table—can give you the extra space you need. That's not to say that larger pieces never work. The couch below is actually oversize, but its neutral color helps it blend in and provides enough seating to earn its keep. In some space-challenged rooms, though, thinking small is the best route. For instance, who says a living room has to have a sofa? A settee (page 29) may be the perfect solution.

Reuse it!

Swap out a regular-size coffee table and replace it with a narrower version to make a small room feel bigger.

Buy it! This tufted settee has an outsize presence, without taking up too much room.

Look Out Below!

When you're thinking of ways to update, don't forget the floor. A natural-fiber rug is a smart choice if you want to make a lot of impact without a lot of fuss. It adds a grounding note to white rooms, brings in texture, and plays well with other natural elements. It can also be an excellent backdrop for a smaller rug that makes a bigger statement—say, a cowhide, a bright wool rug, or an Oriental. In this case, more is more.

Buy it!

Add a woven layer to your living room with a natural fiber rug.

Know Your

NATURAL FIBER RUGS

SEAGRASS is well-suited to the dining room because its super-tight weave makes it difficult for crumbs to hide. (Plus, it's the least bare-foot friendly of the bunch.)

JUTE is good for the living room, thanks to a thicker, nubby weave that can handle high traffic. It's also soft underfoot.

SISAL is excellent for the bedroom. It lies nice and flat, so it's easier to layer softer rugs on top.

Do it!

Slipping a bright white cowhide between the sisal rug and the coffee table adds softness and highlights the conversation zone in front of the fireplace.

Do it! In this updated classic blue living room, rugs in contrasting tones and textures define the seating area and warm up the cool-toned space.

Five Bright Ideas

1. A pair of basic but colorful sofas makes a statement and provides a great backdrop for both pink and yellow pillows at the same time.

2. This appealing chippy green coffee table is actually a dining table cut down to size.

3. Don't be afraid to go bright with small pieces of furniture, like this yellow side table. (It's also a nod to the yellow kitchen island in the next room.)

4. Pink patterned armchairs lend a classy note. The pattern is subtle enough to complement —not clash with—the blue patterned pillows.

5. Indigo patterned curtains pick up the blue of the couches and invite you into the backyard.

Focal Points

Certain places in a living room cry out for objects worthy of attention. The area above the mantel is a natural place for display; the wall above a sofa is another. Take advantage of these spaces to make a splash and your room will be upgraded instantly. If rustic is your style, found objects (like the old window screens on page 37) can take on new life as sculptural pieces when they're given a chance to shine. It's worth thinking big, as large pieces —like the 6-foot-wide wooden horse on this page—make a statement. But a collection of smaller treasured objects— mirrors, silhouettes, portraits, and oils—can be artfully grouped to create a notable gallery wall. And if you don't own anything worth hanging, don't despair. Just keep an eye out for paintings and signs at tag sales and flea markets, and you'll be able to curate a collection for a song.

Buy it!

A large wooden filly adds a graphic, modern touch to this streamlined country living room.

WELCOME
VISITORS
PLEASE
REGISTER
HERE

Reuse it! A vintage camp sign and a collection of floral paintings make it a garden party all year long in this farmhouse living room.

Reuse it! This gallery wall could have looked stuffy, but raw-edged, unframed portraits keep it casual and inviting.

Prized Possessions

Hunting and gathering pieces for a growing collection is a great way to pass a weekend afternoon. But enjoying your finds after you've brought them home is even better. While there's nothing wrong with displaying them throughout the house, a grouping gives you the maximum oomph. In the room on page 41, shelves cleverly built around a bulky, unmovable radiator are home to a collection of white ceramics that's perfectly in keeping with the neutral tones of the room. On this page, a shelf built above the door frame creates an expected place to show off a beautiful collection of green pottery. As a bonus, it lifts the fragile objects out of the path of children and dogs.

Do it!

Green is the theme in this stylish room. The chairs in the living and dining rooms reinforce the shade of the pottery collection on display.

BALDWIN

Do it!

A treasured collection of white pottery anchors one of the living room walls in this Connecticut home.

Ready, Set, Paint!

There's no better way to totally transform a room than to give it a coat of paint. A new color changes everything, whether you apply it to one wall or all of the walls. Make an unexpected update by changing the color of the ceiling or just the ceiling beams, which require both minimum paint and effort. Or paint your walls two different shades to give an otherwise ordinary room vintage flair.

Do it!

The homeowners toned down the traditionally bold-colored walls of this 1850s Victorian home by painting the room white and filling in the walls above the wainscoting with charcoal paint, making the pristine details stand out.

Do it!

In a home filled with exuberant patterns, vibrant turquoise beams and trim are perfectly in sync with the extroverted vibe.

Do it!

Bold aqua-blue paint sets off a white mantel and a dramatic piece of art.

Do it!

An airy pale-blue ceiling above white spruce-plank-clad walls makes this 1970s rancher feel more spacious and less boxy.

BEFORE

Do it! Plaster walls in two blue-gray tones recall an earlier age and are a vast improvement over the previous purple. Plus, the antique sofa and quirky arrangement of vintage botanical prints and oil paintings give the room identity and make it inviting.

CHAPTER 2

Dining Rooms

Whether you have a formal dining room set aside just for dinner or you eat in a more casual space, there are tons of simple ways to make the area fresher, brighter, and more distinctively yours. More than in most rooms, swapping in a new light fixture can instantly change the tone; a chandelier or pendant above the table holds a central place in the room. Letting go of the idea of a table-and-chairs set frees you up to mix and match in a way that reflects your personality. Consider displaying a treasured collection of dishes or whiteware in a hutch (or, if your space is small, a mini dish rack on the wall) or hanging a distinctive piece of artwork, such as the botanical chart on page 73. Architectural details salvaged from old buildings, like mantelpieces or decorative lintels, can add charm and a sense of history. And a bold tablecloth or runner is an almost effortless way to punch up a room with color or graphics—or both. Best of all, you can change a tablecloth anytime you like.

Do it!

The easiest mini makeover of all? Place a bouquet of beautiful flowers on your dining room table. Bonus points: Pick them from your own yard!

Bright Ideas

A light fixture makes a big statement in the dining room. With just one switch, you can nudge your space toward whatever style you like, be it formal, modern, rustic, or something else. In country-style homes, weathered-metal examples are particularly appealing and appropriate, and they are easy to find at all price points. Or you can make your own galvanized tin shades; see pages 56–57.

Buy it!

A notable oversize lampshade hovers above the dining table, which was whittled down from a larger antique piece and paired with a sleek steel frame.

Make it! A Connecticut homeowner gave this black iron chandelier—a flea-market find—a modern punch with black-and-white striped shades, which she added. A little bit of paint is all you need to create this look.

Do it!

For only $40 and some elbow grease, a North Carolina homeowner restored her parents' old porch light and turned it into a handsome dining room pendant.

CARTS

Buy it! A weathered French pendant is a standout in this neutral dining room.

These zinc light fixtures look weathered, but they're actually newly purchased.

Make it!

Galvanized tin pendant lights made from vintage floral buckets carry out this room's garden theme.

Galvanized Pendants

1 Drill a hole in the center of the bottom of the galvanized tin.

2 Then, drill holes around the exterior as an added decorative touch, if desired.

3 Thread the plug end of a pendant light cord set through the hole from the bottom of the tin.

4 Hang the pendant in desired location.

Buy it!

The pendant lights in this farmhouse dining room were crafted from repurposed chicken wire.

Please Be Seated

When it comes to chairs and country style, the more kinds you have, the merrier. Trade your perfectly matched set for anything you like: shabby bentwood numbers or ladder-backs, even a bench. You can paint different styles the same color to help the chairs harmonize, or keep them the way they are and enjoy their individuality. Slipcovers can be added into the mix, too. If you do go for a matched set, search out material that makes a statement: bold-patterned fabric or industrial-influenced steel seats.

Do it!

Distressed bentwood chairs, a picnic bench with a metal crossbar, and a classic ladder-back chair combine nicely in this dining room. Hydrangeas and a neutral table runner add polish.

Do it!

If you're going for a down-home feel, skip the straight-from-the-store dining set and match a rough-hewn farm table (this one was a Craigslist® find) with bentwood chairs collected over time. A comfy wicker armchair makes for the perfect seat at the head of the table.

Do it!

Slipcovers with grain sack–inspired stripes add subtle pattern to a vast white room.

Do it!

Slipcovered chairs along with ladder-backs with upholstered seats provide interest, variety, and welcome light notes in this cypress-paneled Alabama dining room.

Shelf Life

F ull-sized hutches or mini wall-mounted versions, built-in shelving, and china cabinets offer a place to show off treasured collections. They or their displayed objects can bring color to a room (or a wash of white) and loads of personality. Collections needn't be pricey. Artfully arranged tag-sale and flea-market finds work just fine. If you're just beginning to collect, you can accumulate colorful midcentury pieces, look for a theme, or stick to a limited palette for maximum punch.

Do it!

An old-fashioned plate rack mounted on the wall offers the charm of a rustic cupboard for a fraction of the space—and price. Pretty blue-and-white dishware makes the rack a dining-room focal point.

Do it! Vibrant secondhand dishware is shown off in an early nineteenth-century pine hutch.

Do it! Plates with a wild-game theme are distinctive amid white pottery and tinted glassware in this ornate hutch with striking spiral legs.

Do it! Green glassware is pretty and practical on the open shelving above a stainless-steel cabinet topped with concrete.

Hang It Up

Swapping out the wall decor in your dining room is a quick little way to make a big change. Secondhand finds, such as floral paintings and trays, are one way to go. Black is always striking, whether it's the background of a vintage botanical chart (page 73) or just a simple blackboard (page 72). And don't overlook architectural salvage for drama; you don't have to have a fireplace to hang a mantel on the wall!

Do it!

Wallflowers are a good thing in this humble dining room. Grouping flea-market paintings by topic is easy and delivers visual impact.

Do it!

Vintage metal trays accentuate the patterned curtains and take this room's floral theme one step further.

Know Your

COUNTRY PATTERNS

GINGHAM

CHINTZ

STARS

TICKING STRIPE

PAISLEY

Do it!

All-white cabinetry? Indulge in a pattern overhead. Use peel and stick wallpaper for easy application.

Do it!

Many designers will tell you that any room looks better with a touch of black. An oversize chalkboard hits the mark in an interesting and affordable way.

Buy it!

Staples of many a
school classroom, these
statement posters lend
graphic punch to a
room for far less money
than framed art.

Make it! This eclectic dining room, with mismatched chairs and an heirloom chandelier, demanded that something highly personal be hung over the mantel. The homeowner created her own found-art installation composed of "things too pretty to throw away."

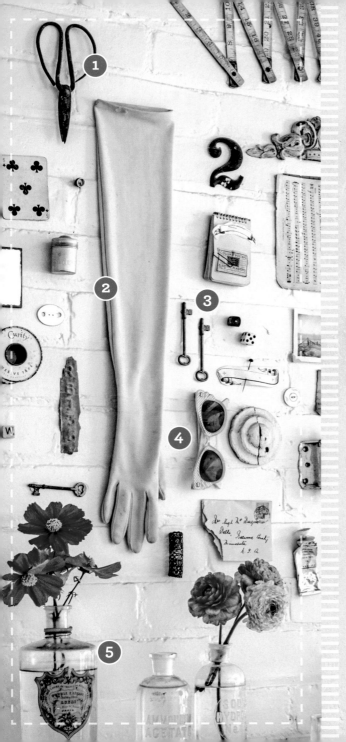

Found-Art Installation

To create a unique assortment of finds, both sentimental and stumbled-upon, be inspired by this stunning arrangement. It contains:

1 Scissors the homeowner came across in a field

2 A vintage glove she wore to her best friend's wedding

3 A couple of old fashioned keys found in a vintage thrift shop

4 Her grandmother's sunglasses

5 Assorted antique medicine and perfume bottles she discovered in her barn, used smartly as bud vases

6 A prize ribbon from her husband's 4-H days (*shown on page 74, top right*)

Reuse it! In this relatively spare dining room, architectural salvage in the form of a mantel and a flea-market find above the window help fill out the space.

Reuse it! Pewter plates liberated from the adjacent china cabinet perfectly complement the soft gray walls of this Georgia dining room.

Four Smart Ideas

1 Make curtains from humble drop cloths. You'll save a bundle!

2 Pair midcentury-inspired metal chairs with a rustic wooden maple dining table. Round it out with vintage pieces for a room that spans decades but looks thoroughly up-to-date.

3 In an awkwardly shaped room, such as this one, you can fool the eye and restore balance by creating symmetry. Here, a slanted fireplace cuts into one corner of the room, resulting in a not-quite-rectangular layout, but the addition of two china cabinets and a pair of coordinating suzani rugs do the trick to even out the space.

4 Conceal clutter in china cabinets by stapling drop cloths inside the lower doors.

Think Small

Reuse it!

A dining table needn't be massive. After all, how often do you have company? If you set up the room for your everyday needs, you'll gain floor space and an airy, open feeling.

Reuse it! In this Northern California dining room, a wicker desk is pressed into service as a dining table.

Do it! A gauzy white tablecloth makes this table for four seem generous in size.

Be Bold

A dining room is no place to shy away from drama. Neutrals are even nicer when they're set off by unexpected colors or statement pieces, such as oversize light fixtures. Refined meets outspoken in these rooms, where an understated table is flanked by eye-catching chairs (and vice versa).

Do it!

Beech bentwood chairs lacquered in apple green and a giant antler chandelier give this neutral dining room distinction.

Buy it! Basic black is bold in this dining room, where new Windsor-style chairs flank an antique table and a black metal pendant lamp hangs above.

A checkerboard-patterned floor original to the house accents periwinkle chairs and a china cabinet in the same hue.

Do it! Go Old World! An Oriental rug anchors a room that boasts an antique table (complete with drawers for napkins), folding camp chairs outfitted with grain sack–covered cushions, a gold chandelier painted white, and a chippy green sideboard.

Thinking Out-of-the-Box

Whether the goal is saving money or creating a distinctive room, it's always smart to look beyond the usual suspects. For example, outdoor furniture can work just as well inside, and odds and ends can be pressed into service in surprising ways!

Bargain!

Why splurge on a dining room table when you can repurpose a basic picnic table instead? Covered with a neutral tablecloth and placemats on top, this unfinished wood table fits right into the dining room setting.

Make it! Look closely: The built-in banquettes in this dining area are simply kitchen cabinets (left over from the kitchen renovation) turned on their sides. And they provide extra storage for a bonus!

CHAPTER 3

Bedrooms

Probably the most private rooms in your home, bedrooms sometimes lose out in favor of more public areas when it comes to decorating. If yours could use a tweak or two, you're not alone. Quilts, coverlets, pillows, and linens—whether coordinating or contrasting—can go a long way toward making a bedroom look pulled together. No formal headboard? No worries. We have many ideas for easy alternatives that may be even better than the real thing. And be sure to add a couple of bedside tables—we've got some suggestions that are just right, even if you're a little short on space. Consider dark wall colors to create cozy spaces. Or opt for light, bright, and cheerful. The choice is yours!

Do it!

Don't be afraid
to go all white—
but add interest
and texture to
otherwise
understated
bedding with
pleats, pin tucks,
and stitching.
Spindle posts on
the bed frame
provide a touch
of elegance.

Bright & Cheery

While white, or neutral, creates a serene space, playing with color presents all kinds of options for mixing and matching shades and patterns. Soothing blue is a natural hue for a sleeping area and works well as a room's primary pigment. In country-style homes, bright painted headboards and colorful quilts are a time-honored combination. Floral patterns and stripes in vibrant colors are another way to go.

Do it!

This bold blue bedroom offers three easy upgrades worth borrowing: a striking blue velvet coverlet, a painted bedstead, and patterned wallpaper.

Do it! Blue has "checks appeal" in this bedroom, where the headboard, bed skirt, and carpet all display the pattern. Walls, curtains, linens, and even the bench at the foot of the bed are blue as well, creating a pleasing background where white accents—like the lamp, the knobs on the chest, and the arms and legs of the chair—really pop.

Do it!   In this bedroom, more is more when it comes to country patterns—buffalo-check curtains and grain-sack fabric on the armchair and pillow complement a vintage blue-and-white quilt.

Reuse it! A pinwheel quilt is elevated from bedcover to striking wall hanging and becomes the focal point of the room. It's balanced by a bright-green-and-white patterned rug.

Know Your

◇

FLORALS

DITSY

A small-scale, random, allover pattern.

BOUQUET OF BLOOMS

A bold multifloral fabric, often a starting point for a room's palette.

SINGLE FLOWER

A single bloom on a repeat that makes a major graphic statement.

Do it!

To put together a bright, patterned room like this one, start with a large-scale floral print—in this case, the coverlet —and complement with small-scale prints (the curtains and the gingham pillow). With so many patterns in the mix, we suggest providing an understated background, such as the whitewashed headboard and white wood-paneled walls.

Painting Stripes in Six Easy Steps

1. To re-create the statement-making look on this page, start by painting your walls the lighter of two selected colors. Wait roughly four hours until the paint dries completely.

2. Starting in a corner of the room, use a piece of blue chalk to place a light mark where each stripe should fall (the stripes here are 6 inches wide).

3. Next, using a level as your guide, draw floor-to-ceiling lines with the blue chalk.

4. Next, line painter's tape along the chalk lines with the tape inside the stripe that will stay the lighter wall color.

5. Paint the darker color between tape strips.

6. Remove tape shortly after painting to ensure the dried paint will not peel from the walls.

Do it!

The festive stripes in the play area of this child's bedroom set the tone for hours of fun. Brown and white stripes painted on the wall mirror the blue-and-white rug, and paint-splatter wallpaper on the ceiling adds subtle whimsy.

Beds & Boards

The bed is the focal point of any bedroom, but you don't have to go with something ready-made. Creating your own headboard makes the room personal. You can work with fabric, found objects, or even forgo a headboard altogether in favor of an open window and a gentle breeze.

Do it!

In this rustic older home, gauzy curtains and an open window are the perfect substitute for a headboard.

Do it!

BONUS! *This piece doubles as a memo board.*

Bonne Nuit

Reuse it! In this snug space, a twin bed is pushed up against the wall with just enough room for a green chalkboard in place of a headboard.

Reuse it!

The shutter hanging above the bed in this Rhode Island home complements the mix of rustic and traditional details in the room.

—'twas grace that taught my heart to fear, and grace my fears relieved— How precious did that grace appear the Hour I first believed.

Make it! A thrifty homeowner rescued a pair of Mexican pine doors, painted them with a gray glaze, and nailed them together for a stylish headboard.

Reuse it! These tin panels were meant as a temporary headboard, but they worked so well that they were never replaced!

Little Wonders

I t's hard to imagine anything cozier or more inviting than a canopy bed. And there are easy ways to make (or fake) your own.

Make it!

Extra-long curtains perform a double-duty function as a canopy. Hung from a bed crown above the windows, the curtain-canopy adds a dramatic touch to a tucked-away attic bedroom.

Make it! This pretty canopy, made of windowpane-plaid fabric panels hung from a frame of simple crown molding, fills the master bedroom with soft texture.

Mix it Up!

Combining stripes, plaid, florals, and other country patterns in textiles (like bedding and rugs) along with pleasing solid colors makes a room vibrant. Stick to the same color family, or add a contrasting shade, such as the red quilt at the foot of the bed on the next page.

Do it!

In this New England home, twin beds are outfitted with striped duvets, checked pillows, and small-scale floral patterned sheets. A classic plaid rug pulls the space all together.

For a bed that's crisply made, try the simple tactic of using three covers—a neutral coverlet, a patterned duvet, and a colorful quilt— layering one atop the other. Starting at the base of the pillow shams, leave roughly a third of each blanket exposed.

Four Clever Ideas

1. To save the expense and headache of wallpaper, use fabric. First roll liquid starch directly on the walls. Then mount the fabric and apply a second coat of starch for extra adhesion.

2. For easy wall art, raid the china cabinet and mount an assortment of plates above the headboard.

3. Craft a pretty bolster pillow from a vintage grain sack. This one bears the initials of the original owner.

4. Upgrade a discarded storage cabinet with an ornate stencil and use it as a bedside table.

On the Wall

Bedroom "art" needn't be fancy. Thrift-store finds, homemade creations, old sports equipment, or plates (as on pages 108–109) are all fair game.

Reuse it!

This gallery wall forgoes a formal grid and has a looser feeling. To create this look in your home, pick an overarching concept or color that ties the artwork together (such as pressed botanicals in a palette of black, white, and tan, as shown here). Then start at the center of the wall with your favorite piece as a focal point and work outward, varying the size and shape of each piece.

Make it! The garden feeling of bold green walls is enhanced by lattice (purchased at a home-improvement store like Home Depot®) and applied using a nail gun. An array of paper flowers completes the theme.

Charming artwork can be found in everyday objects. The dapper dog prints above this boy's bed are simply enlarged note cards!

Dark & Cozy

ark walls in a bedroom make the space seem snug yet inviting. Deep greens, grays, and other saturated shades can work well in small rooms and large ones, too.

Do it! The rich green paint in this room accentuates a four-poster spindle bed, the striped blanket on the bed, and the botanical curtains.

Do it! In this room, both the walls and the ceiling are painted a dark shade, which makes the white bedding and flooring pop.

Do it!

When the new homeowners removed the wallpaper in this room (see inset photo), they discovered a verdant antique-green shade of milk paint. They decided to keep the walls "as is" for an age-old vibe.

BEFORE

Window Dressing

Plain curtains are inexpensive and work well in most rooms. Kick them up a notch by decorating them with upholstery tape or ribbon if your room requires more punch.

Do it!

Indigo upholstery tape adds appeal to pinch-pleat linen curtains. The placement of this accent also draws the eye to the ornate bedside table in this subtly patterned bedroom.

Do it! Basic ready-made curtains take a luxurious turn when trimmed with 2-inch-wide grosgrain or a heavy, stiff-ribbed ribbon.

On the Side

When it comes to bedside tables, it pays to experiment. A smaller room may not have the space for the classic type, and there are so many other ways to go. Old luggage, chairs, and boxes can all be pressed into service for nightstands that are attractive and practical.

Do it!

Steamer-trunks-turned-nightstand add charm to the room—and provide storage to boot!

Do it! In this tiny room, "floating" surfaces stand in for bedside tables, and—along with the striking orange-patterned horizontal pillow and the parallel wood beams in the ceiling—help draw the eye out and make the space seem wider.

Reuse it! In this small bedroom, a ghost chair (left) and old ballot box (right) serve as mismatched nightstands. Sconce lighting on each side of the bed frees up the tables' surfaces for books and a pretty stand mirror.

Do it!

This pretty metal nightstand is suspended from the ceiling and keeps the pale-blue room looking light and airy.

Step on It

Painted floors result in instant country charm and can make quite a statement. Solid colors are lovely, and painting a pattern may be easier to pull off than you suspect.

Do it!

Painting floors a bold color, like the cobalt blue here, pulls a room together. Plus, it is cheaper than refinishing well-loved wooden floors.

Do it! Turquoise and green squares unify a bedroom suite that includes two bedrooms and a bathroom. Ultra-durable Break-Through!® paint, typically used for garage floors, dries in less than an hour, which makes applying two-tone patterns much easier.

Rough & Ready

Not everything in a bedroom has to be soft. Rough-hewn furniture, found signage, and barn-inspired details are right at home in farmhouses and cabins.

Do it!

A salvaged railroad sign and sliding barn door are perfect for a small boy's room—and won't look childish as he grows older

Reuse it! A former park bench installed at the foot of the bed provides another surface for personal items and echoes the rustic feeling of the wooden ceiling beams.

CHAPTER 4

Kitchens & Baths

Hardworking kitchens and baths tend to need more TLC than other rooms in the house, which means they're ready candidates for little touch-ups. Clever organizing and storage solutions can make a big difference, as can ingenious ideas for sprucing up backsplashes, pantries, and other kitchen essentials. Switching up seating, wall and cabinet colors (country kitchens don't have to be white!), flooring, and wall decor are other relatively easy ways to breathe new life into a tired room. And don't forget the bath! This small area works 24/7 but can convey a lot of personality, too. Our easy upgrades will show you how to add storage, light, and a sense of space.

Do it!

In an otherwise neutral kitchen, a built-in cabinet is painted a remarkable robin's-egg blue. Chalkboard paint transforms a cabinet door into a message center for the family.

Cover-Ups

Not everything in a kitchen should be seen as is. Areas under sinks or countertops that haven't been outfitted with cabinetry can be disguised economically and charmingly with fabric curtains. Self-adhesive shelf paper is the solution for appliances or cabinets that have seen better days. And backsplashes can be gussied up with tile, of course, but also with fabric or wallpaper. As for windows, café curtains are a simple and classic way to go, and they may not even require sewing!

Make it!

To veil an under-the-sink storage area with no cabinets, the homeowner cut and tied linen to an old café curtain rod. This decorating technique can also be used in bathrooms to hide extra supplies!

Make it!

Burlap skirts conceal plywood shelves stocked with pots and pans.

Do it! In this white kitchen, a white appliance looked too bland. To warm it up—and mix it up—the homeowner applied wallpaper to the refrigerator using wallpaper paste and, for water resistance, sealed it with polyurethane.

Do it! Cabinets can be improved with contact paper, too—inside and out. Beadboard backing in the open shelves gives this kitchen a country vibe. Best of all, it's easy to remove when you're ready for a change.

Do it!

Tile is the classic backsplash material, and a sunny pattern adds interest to a pretty, quiet kitchen.

Do it! A full-scale kitchen renovation is in this homeowner's long-term plans, but until then, a beadboard-inspired wallpaper backsplash is economical, water-resistant, and easy to remove. Plus, it's just as charming as the real deal.

Do it!

Cook up charming café curtains by sewing a strip of rickrack along the bottom—or spiff up humble dish towels with crisscrossed lengths secured with fusible bonding tape.

Make it! No sewing is required to create these charming café curtains! Use a seam ripper to remove the seam stitching from a grain sack. Unfold the fabric and trim to fit the measurements of the window. (Grain-sack fabric is usually so sturdy that it makes for a clean cut—no hemming necessary.) Lastly, hang it from a drapery rod using curtain clips.

Get Organized

I n a room as busy as a kitchen, everything needs a place. Baskets, bins, shelves, and even hanging pegs can all be pressed into service.

Do it!

Vintage wire baskets set atop a custom-built wooden shelf and iron-frame structure store linens, dishes, and pantry items in an organized, at-a-glance fashion.

Do it!

Hang pots within easy reach. This Vermont homeowner fashioned a pot rack by mounting a 2×2—painted the same color as the beam—overhead. Sturdy hooks hold heavy cast-iron pans for quick access.

Know Your

SHELF SUPPORTS

MODERN

RUSTIC

CLASSIC

INDUSTRIAL

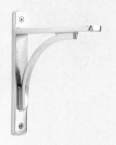

POLISHED

Do it!

Open shelving is a hallmark of a farmhouse kitchen and doubles as storage and display.

Perfect Pantries

Who doesn't covet a gorgeous, organized larder filled to the brim with everything you could possibly need to put wonderful meals on the table? If your house didn't come with one built in, there are plenty of work-arounds, such as the two appealing options shown here.

Reuse it!

If you don't have an integrated pantry, look for stand-alone storage. This armoire-turned-cupboard is right on trend, and you can add or remove shelves to suit your needs.

142

Reuse it!

Any utilitarian shelving system can be put to creative uses. Just outfit it with breathable baskets to corral everything from various types of produce to bulky bags of dry goods, like flour and sugar.

Do it!

Upgrade a pantry with barn door–inspired panels mounted on a flat-track hardware set.

This pantry was a dark, small space, but painted white, it serves as the perfect backdrop for the homeowner's collection of vintage jadeite dishes.

BREAD

CANADA DRY

Reuse it!

Come on in! A screen door from a big-box store that was painted bright green shows the way to the pantry.

1 EASIEST

3 EASY-ISH

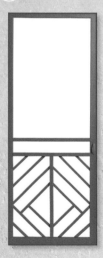

2 EASY

EASY CRAFT

Spruce Up a Screen Door

Here are three ways to trick out a plain screen door:

1 EASIEST Use screws and headers to attach decorative trim—no saw or drill needed.

2 EASY Use a hacksaw to cut ¾-inch square dowels to create panes, and attach four fan brackets to make a circle. Add a gallery rail and spandrel for horizontal strips.

3 EASY-ISH Use a chop saw to cut two 36 × ¾-inch dowels at 45° angles, and place them as shown.

Living Color

There's no doubt about it: White is the go-to pigment for a farmhouse kitchen. But it doesn't have to be that way, and we've got proof. Just check out the shades on the next few pages: pales, brights, darks, even crazy patterns. They all work wonderfully!

Do it!

Rather than go with unpainted wooden cabinets in this cabin, the homeowners opted for a warm grayish white that creates an airy swathe among the dark wood paneling in surrounding rooms.

Do it! The island, painted a crisp shade of yellowy green, pairs beautifully with a bold blue-tile backsplash in a repeating quilt-like pattern.

Do it! The owners of this home painted the kitchen's ceiling a dreamy shade of blue and covered the walls in a classically country paper featuring milk jugs and teacups.

_Do it!_ Bright green stands out against a white farmhouse sink and pristine marble countertops and makes a bold statement in this pared-down kitchen.

Do it! Buttery-colored walls provide a soft backdrop for weathered turquoise cabinetry. Red-accented decor, like the stand mixer, casserole dish, knobs on the stove, timer, and marquee-lit arrow, really pops.

152

Do it! Enveloping the room in this strong sapphire-inspired shade makes it less shocking and more welcoming than a single outrageous dose would. Sunny Mexican-inspired tiles wake up the backsplash.

Do it! Black cabinets and walls blend together for a polished, seamless look.

TOURISTS

Marché aux fleurs

Do it! A chalkboard wall makes a big design impact in this kitchen—
and it's a fun place to leave notes for your family or roommates.

Illuminating Statements

Lighting is important in a kitchen, but that doesn't mean you have to sacrifice style for function. The options on these pages are practical beauties that also further each room's design.

Buy it!

The new pendant light in this antiques-filled kitchen looks as if it's been hanging around for centuries.

Two oversize galvanized fixtures above the teak island emphasize this beach home's casual vibe.

 Reuse it! Repurposed as light shades, nubby 2-foot-tall baskets add texture and offer up plenty of illumination for kitchen tasks.

158

Do it! The basket pendant lights in this roomy kitchen add warmth and interest. And check out the rope-covered support post nearby, which provides more rustic charm.

Floor Models

Whether you choose to go with a patterned floor or a solid shade, what's underfoot has an impact on a room's design.

Do it!

A green-and-blue pattern inspired by an Ohio star quilt is painted on this kitchen floor.

Do it! The natural-wood and white-painted diamonds on the floor echo the mix of materials found throughout this kitchen (combinations like wood and marble countertops and bronze and brass hardware), which result in a rich, layered feeling.

Do it!

This classic white kitchen warms up with a dark stain on the wooden floor.

Six Fun Ideas

It's possible to have a vibrant, happy kitchen that embraces multiple colors without sacrificing cohesion. Take a look:

1 Show off collectibles by lining built-ins with peel-and-stick contact paper in a pretty pattern.

2 Give white cabinetry a subtle kick of color with red knobs (or other colors or patterns).

3 Go for a colorful kettle. Just because it's utilitarian doesn't mean it can't add to the decor!

4 Choose a range in a showstopping, unexpected color like this light-blue one.

5 Paint a checkerboard floor! Choose hues that are near each other on the color wheel (pink and red, yellow and orange, green and blue as shown here). If the colors are too high contrast, the combo could have a vibrating effect. For spaces smaller than 12 × 12 feet, try an 18-inch square; for larger spaces, go with 24 inches.

6 It's island time! A bright-red X-braced island holds court in the center of the room.

Sitting Pretty

Choosing seating for a kitchen island is a chance to reinforce the room's design theme—or take it in a complementary direction.

Make it!

Old shirts from the local thrift store find new life as bespoke stool toppers in this rustic kitchen.

Reuse it! Red tractor seats and vintage vinyl barstools pair up as seating for this salvaged island, originally a counter in a New Jersey general store.

Buy it!

Freshen up farmhouse style by adding something unexpected. Sleek iron bar stools covered in pale-aqua patent leather offer a cool, modern counterpart to traditional country kitchen touches like a butcher-block island, subway-tile backsplash, and an apron-front sink.

Light Touches

In an upstairs bath, privacy is usually less of a concern, so curtains can let in some light. Gauzy fabrics fill the bill, and café curtains hung at half-mast let even more sunshine stream in.

Do it!

A yard of cheesecloth hung from Shaker pegs above the window adds a soft, feminine finish that complements the tub.

Do it! The white curtains, walls, and claw-foot tub are balanced by a striking mahogany china cabinet and warm Turkish rug in this charming bathroom

Vanity Project

Mirrors create the illusion of more space, and a lot of mirrors create the illusion of a lot more space! Besides, where are mirrors more appropriate than in a bathroom?

Do it!

In this small bathroom, mirrors of all shapes and sizes hung gallery-style throughout the room practically double the sense of space.

A collection of vintage mirrors—some shaving mirrors and one salvaged from an old car—is showcased on the sink counter in this bath.

Hold It!

Towels, soaps, bath clothes, toilet paper—bathrooms are brimming with things you use up quickly, so it's smart to have backups close at hand. Bins and baskets on tables, toilet backs, and floors, under the sink, or even on the wall are easy ways to go.

Reuse it!

Turn hatboxes into bathroom storage to free up bathroom drawers and counter space. Just choose boxes that are 10 to 12 inches deep, add peppy color to boot, and then nail the backs to the wall.

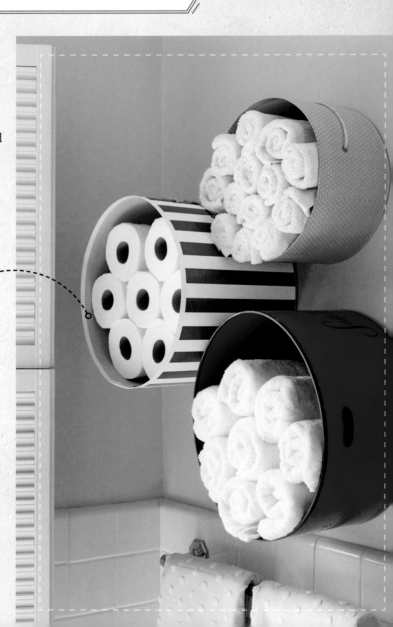

Reuse it! An antique basket tucked beneath a dresser-turned-vanity is another way to hold towels, extra soaps, and toilet paper.

Reuse it!

A vintage persimmons crate corrals towels in this old desk—now topped with marble and doing service as a bathroom vanity.

Reuse it! Sweet idea! Use a sugar mold to contain toiletries and makeup tools. Thanks to a slim profile, a mold will fit easily on a window ledge or countertop.

Real Country

A little creative thinking can bring rural charm to a modern bath. Go beyond the farmhouse sink and consider using honest-to-goodness farm equipment as a sink, as in the photo below. Or take a more refined tack and search out shabby-chic painted furniture and unusual fixtures.

Reuse it!

In this rustic bath, a simple wood stand (with holes drilled for plumbing) transforms a Dutch galvanized-metal hay-collecting bin into a statement-making sink.

Reuse it!

In a small downstairs bath, pops of green, such as the jadeite towel bar and the appealing mirror, enliven the pristine white space.

Little Touches

Delight is in the details—they're what give a room warmth and character. Whether personal, like photos (or silhouettes) or quirky nods to hobbies or location, sharing a little bit of yourself makes all the difference.

Do it!

Silhouettes—some of the household's children, others of strangers—rest on bold plaid wallpaper that's juxtaposed to an ornately carved wooden mirror.

Reuse it! A lifesaver on the wall and ship atop the towel-filled armoire bring a jaunty nautical note to this inviting white bath. White towels with navy stripes add to the all-aboard air.

CHAPTER 5

Small Spaces

Homes are full of all kinds of smaller spaces that can make memorable statements with just a little investment. Petite sitting rooms, alcoves fitted with daybeds or window seats, or the area beneath a staircase are cozy places just right for curling up with a book or for a nap. Entryways, stairways, and home offices are other places that can benefit from interesting art, textured fabrics, and unexpected shades of paint on the walls. Mudrooms and porches—spaces in the home that walk the line between out and in—are often overlooked areas where stylish touches go a long, long way.

Buy it! Striking reproduction shipyard lanterns equipped with battery-operated candles illuminate this quaint sitting room.

Nooks That Say . . .

Nap, or settle in with a book, or have an intimate conversation—these little areas can add another dimension to a home, making it feel bigger than it really is. Make sure these spaces are comfy, with cushions, throws, and rugs, or a place to put your feet up. After a mini makeover, one of these spots may become your favorite place in your home!

Do it!

A colorful cushion atop a low-slung cabinet fits perfectly into an alcove beside the fireplace, and results in an inviting place to curl up with your laptop.

Do it! An unused corner becomes a go-to spot when outfitted with a daybed constructed from flea market–found doors and pallets, and pillowcases made from old grain sacks. Cushy cubes say "put your feet up," and sconces made from cow-feed sifters disseminate light.

Do it! There's no mistaking the purpose of this corner of an enclosed porch. A floor-to-ceiling stack of books and ceiling fixtures made from tomes no one would miss make it perfectly clear it's for reading!

Do it! This under-the-stairs spot was once a closet with book storage on one side. With doors removed, it's now a little library—and a good place for a heart-to-heart conversation.

Come On In

Entryways are often minuscule spaces, but they have an impact way out of proportion to their size. They provide an important first look into your home and can be a place to drop coats, keys, and totes when you arrive home.

Reuse it!

A stack of vintage luggage adds decorative oomph to a hallway while providing twelve "drawers" of storage for out-of-season pieces.

Reuse it! A rustic table hosts a welcoming bar and is highlighted by an off-black wall. Underneath, a vintage suitcase and a woven trunk store extra drinking glasses.

Reuse it!

A bottle drying rack serves as a hardworking organizer in this entryway.

Reuse it! Flea-market mirrors atop a carpenter's-workbench-turned-console set an in-with-the-old tone.

EASY CRAFT

Decoupage Dresser

Revive an old piece with botanicals following these easy instructions:

1 Make paper photocopies of a botanical fabric, then use a utility knife to cut out desired portions of the print.

2 With dresser drawers closed and pulls removed, map out the placement of each botanical.

3 When the design is fully planned, begin to decoupage each piece to the dresser using a medium-strength all-in-one adhesive like Mod Podge®.

4 Once dry, carefully run a razor blade between drawers so they open properly.

5 Finish with a coat of clear acrylic sealant.

Do it!

Chairs are covered in the same pattern used to create the dresser motif.

 A functional but striking red armoire is right at home in the entryway of this lake house. Bird-bedecked wallpaper echoes the home's natural setting.

Pretty and practical: Up top, this blonde table is all show, with paintings propped against the wall and topiaries in shiny pots. Below, repurposed buckets and baskets hold the stuff of everyday life, such as shoes and knitted throws.

Do it! Bring a little of the outdoors in at any time of year to make a welcoming statement in your entryway. Here, the homeowner has simply placed a branch of colorful autumn leaves in a crystal vase.

Reuse it! The drama of a foyer with black walls and white wainscoting is furthered by a gorgeous white armoire.

Stare-Worthy

Y ou can do a lot more with stairs than cover them with a runner and call it a day. There's no end to the creative fun you can have with a paintbrush or contact paper—just take a look at the ideas on these pages for starters. Think beyond the usual for bannisters and artwork as well.

Do it!

Trellis wallpaper lining the stair treads adds a modern motif to this entryway's many weathered finds.

Do it! Floral wallpaper set off by stairs and railings painted a high-gloss beige lead the way to the second story memorably.

Do it! Display a collection—like these treasured silhouettes—in a stairwell and you can enjoy it multiple times every day.

Retro metal signs, many of them collected at the World's Largest Yard Sale, are the perfect decorations for this stairwell made from reclaimed barnwood (some areas still feature washes of nostalgic red paint).

Stairway Stripes

1. Starting at the top of the landing, paint a wide band (we recommend three-quarters the width of the treads) down the length of staircase.

2. Once dry, tape off three center stripes. Paint them your desired color.

3. When the paint is dry, remove the tape completely.

Do it!

Grain sack–inspired stripes go right up to the second floor!

Do it! Stencil numbers on plywood, then nail them to the stair risers for a playful, graphic look.

Do it!

The stairway railing is made from wire cattle panels purchased at a farm store. Rope will also have the same rustic effect.

Make It Work

More and more of us need a work space at home, but figuring out where to put one isn't always easy. Check out the two clever ideas shown here: a desk nestled into an open living area and another one on the landing at the top of the stairs. If you do have a designated room for an office, consider a soothing dark color and clever organizational tools made from flea-market finds.

Do it!

This home office is squeezed in between the front door and the refrigerator. The desk blends in because it's painted the same color as the walls, and a piece of barnwood covers the side of the stainless steel fridge beside the desk.

THE FRENCH HÔTELS

Do it!

Place a salmon-hued vintage table, an old church pew, and a white-painted chair in a top-of-the-stairs alcove and—voilà—you've got a home office.

Do it! A vibrant navy paint job makes this 8 × 10-foot office feel cozy rather than claustrophobic.

Reuse it! This showstopping memo board started out in life as a bedspring.

With its many tiny compartments, this vintage mail sorter
makes for a first-class desk organizer.

Globe Light

Make it!

Give your office a worldly vibe with this globe light you can make yourself!

1 To create your own pendant, you'll need a 12-inch-diameter cardboard globe (as little as $15 online), plus a pendant-light cord kit.

2 First, remove the globe from its base, if necessary. With a utility knife, carefully make a 3½-inch-diameter opening at the bottom of your globe, using its latitude lines as a guide.

3 Then, holding the light cord's socket at the top of the globe, trace around it with a pencil and cut out the resulting circle.

4 Using a drill fitted with a ⅛-inch bit, pierce small holes around the outline of each continent, leaving ¼ inch between the holes.

5 Insert the socket at the top, following the kit's instructions, then screw in a 15-watt compact fluorescent light bulb from the bottom and hang to display.

Come Clean

If your home came with a mudroom, lucky you! If not, you can create one near an entryway with the addition of racks with pegs for coats, hats, and bags; a bench for removing shoes and boots; and perhaps a tray for storing them.

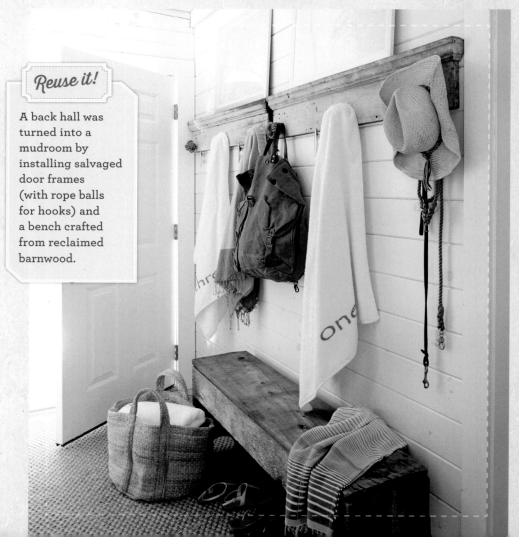

Reuse it!

A back hall was turned into a mudroom by installing salvaged door frames (with rope balls for hooks) and a bench crafted from reclaimed barnwood.

Reuse it!

Jar-drying racks are used as chandeliers in this multipurpose laundry, mudroom, and art studio.

Do it!

A practical yet refined mushroom shade adds a bit of sophistication to this hardworking mudroom.

Do it! The coatrack in this mudroom is made of large sewing spools hammered into a painted board. The family's boots are corralled on a copper tray to prevent dirt from being tracked throughout the house.

Step Outside

Neither outdoors nor in, porches straddle the line between public and private and between nature and shelter. In warmer months, you want to enjoy them as much as you possibly can! So it pays to make them comfortable, welcoming, and attractive, with clever ideas, lots of plants, and upcycled furniture.

Do it!

The graphic black-and-white pattern painted on the floor makes this narrow porch seem wider.

Reuse it!

This porch coffee table is simply a vintage champagne crate topped with glass.

Four Fresh Ideas

This pretty blue porch is brimming with creative concepts:

1 The blue ceiling is inspired by the Gullah culture of South Carolina, where the shade was said to keep evil spirits away. Here it sets a happy vibe.

2 Why exile hanging plants to the porch's perimeter? On this porch, they form a pleasingly random pattern.

3 A white curtain hung at one end of the porch creates privacy and a sense of coziness.

4 An outdoor rug in a pretty blue pattern pulls the space together.

Colander Planters

Vintage colanders in cheery colors make a perfect pot for a hanging plant.

1 Wrap one colander handle tightly with ½ yard of twine, pushing it together as you go to avoid gaps.

2 Once covered, tie off the twine and add a dab of glue to secure.

3 Knot a yard of twine at each end of the handle. Repeat the entire process with the opposite handle.

4 Line the colander with sheet moss and fill with potting soil and seasonal plants (like the pansies and ferns pictured here).

5 Tie the four lengths of twine together and hang the planter.

Index

NOTE: *Page references to photos indicate location of photo captions.*